D1518490

ANIMALS ATTACK!

Piranhas

Nathan Aaseng

KIDHAVEN PRESS

An imprint of Thomson Gale, a part of The Thomson Corporation

THOMSON

━━━━━✦━━━━━™

GALE

Detroit • New York • San Francisco • San Diego • New Haven, Conn. • Waterville, Maine • London • Munich

For more information, contact
KidHaven Press
27500 Drake Rd.
Farmington Hills, MI 48331-3535
Or you can visit our Internet site at http://www.gale.com

LIBRARY OF CONGRESS CATALOGING-IN-PUBLICATION DATA
Aaseng, Nathan.
Piranhas / by Nathan Aaseng.
p. cm. — (Animals attack)
Includes bibliographical references.
ISBN 0-7377-3130-3 (hard cover : alk. paper)
1. Piranhas—Juvenile literature. I. Title. II. Series.
QL638.C5A27 2005
597'.48—dc22
2005007789

Printed in the United States of America

Contents

Chapter 1

Deadliest Fish or Fake Monster?

From the **rain forests** of South America have come terrifying reports of a nightmare come to life. That living nightmare is a meat-eating fish called a piranha. Not only can piranhas kill and eat humans, they can do so with amazing speed. A hungry school of piranhas could strip every ounce of flesh off a person within a matter of minutes, leaving nothing but bones.

Stories of vicious piranha attacks are so disturbing and so widespread that the fish is known throughout the world. It may well be the most feared freshwater creature that has ever lived.

Deadly Fish or Fake Monster?

But are the stories true? Is the piranha really as dangerous as its reputation? Even scientists have had trouble answering these questions over the years. Fish experts once proclaimed that the piranha "may be the most dangerous fish in the world,"[1] because of the number of people it attacked and killed. On the other hand, a respected researcher recently wrote, "It is unlikely that the fish would intentionally attack a larger, living mammal."[2]

Much of the confusion about piranhas comes because they thrive in remote areas of the Amazon River and the waters that flow into it. Human contact with the fish, therefore, has occurred mostly

With its razor-sharp teeth and lightning-fast speed the piranha is one of the most feared creatures on the planet.

among people who have kept no written records or photographs and have communicated little with the outside world.

More confusion arises because there are several dozen **species** of piranhas, and they do not all act the same. Only a few species of piranhas appear to be dangerous. These are distinguished by their colorful bellies, which are usually red but may sometimes be orange or yellow. Even these dangerous piranhas are highly unpredictable. There is no sure way of knowing exactly when and why a piranha will attack.

Clear proof of deadly piranha attacks on humans may be lacking. Experts insist that piranhas seldom, if ever, intentionally attack humans. Yet

Hunting for food, this hungry school of piranhas can devour even very large prey in a matter of seconds.

there are many people walking around with scars from piranha bites. In fact, attacks by piranhas on humans appear to be increasing. In 2004, dozens of swimmers were attacked on a single stretch of river in Brazil within a matter of a few weeks.

Why Are They Dangerous?

Piranhas are small fish that seldom grow longer than 12 inches (30cm) or heavier than 3 pounds (1.4kg). They are thin from side to side and have large, blunt heads. The way their lower jaws jut out farther than their upper jaws causes them to look something like a bulldog. What makes them dangerous are the razor-sharp, triangular teeth that fill those powerful jaws. The name *piranha*, in fact, comes from two words: *pirá*, meaning "fish," and *ana*, meaning "tooth." Often, piranhas have two rows of these teeth. These teeth can slice through bone or nip a neat chunk from the tough hide of a caiman (a relative of the crocodile).

Piranhas are strong swimmers. Faster than the blink of an eye, a piranha can inflict a wound that takes months to heal.

The frightening part about the fish is what they can do in large numbers. Recently, workers at an aquarium in Kazakhstan lowered an ox heart into a tank containing 500 hungry piranhas. The fish completely devoured the heart within five seconds.

One reason for an attack is extreme hunger. The legends of the bloodthirsty piranha are largely due

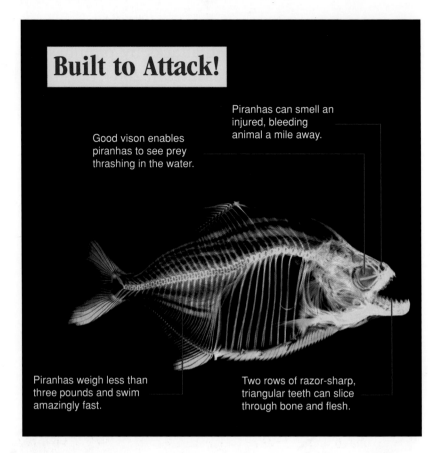

Built to Attack!

Good vison enables piranhas to see prey thrashing in the water.

Piranhas can smell an injured, bleeding animal a mile away.

Piranhas weigh less than three pounds and swim amazingly fast.

Two rows of razor-sharp, triangular teeth can slice through bone and flesh.

to an account written by former U.S. president Theodore Roosevelt. On his Amazon expedition in 1914, he described a wounded cow being driven into a river. The piranhas attacked it with such fury that some leaped out of the water with flesh in their mouths. Within minutes, the cow was a skeleton. What the stunned Roosevelt did not know was that his hosts had staged the event. They closed off a 100-yard (90m) section of river with nets and filled it with piranhas. The fish were not fed for a week. By the time the cow was driven in, the fish were desperately hungry.

Piranhas are known to be especially dangerous during the dry season. Fish trapped in shrinking ponds where they can find no food are especially **aggressive**.

Handle with Care

Most people in the world have no reason to fear a piranha attack. The fish do not survive well outside a tropical environment and are largely restricted to areas that few people visit. Even in piranha-infested rivers, the fish usually avoid people whenever possible. There are many villagers in South America who wade and swim with no fear every day in rivers among piranha populations.

Most piranha injuries happen to people who go out of their way to encounter these fish. Some experts, in fact, believe that more piranha injuries occur outside the rivers where the fish live than in them. Careless handling by fishers probably accounts for the vast majority of injuries. A piranha caught on a hook or placed in unfamiliar surroundings such as a fish tank will defend itself by striking at anything that moves. No one can even guess how many such piranha attacks take place during a year. But travelers such as Keith Sutton note that most river guides in piranha-infested waters have scars from piranha teeth, and most admit they got them by handling piranhas.

Because of their bloodthirsty reputation, piranhas are popular attractions at public aquariums, and many people buy them as pets. Every year, there are dozens of reports of missing fingertips and chunks of flesh from people who underestimated the speed of a piranha attack.

Feeding Frenzy

Piranha attacks can also be triggered by a **feeding frenzy**. While the fish do not often live in large schools, they may be attracted from far off by the prospect of food. Like sharks, piranhas have a keen sense of smell and can detect blood from over a mile (nearly 2km) away. They also have good vision and appear to be especially stimulated by thrashing in the water.

When sight or smell attracts at least twenty piranhas, the entire group may go into a feeding frenzy. During such a frenzy, piranhas will snap at anything that moves, including each other. Researchers say that the fish act as if they are intoxicated and have no control over their actions. Anyone who so much as dips a finger in the water at such a time takes a huge risk. Even those who wade fearlessly among piranhas every day would not dream of entering the water with an open wound that might trigger a feeding frenzy.

Protecting Their Nests

Finally, piranhas are especially likely to attack during their breeding season. After they deposit their eggs, usually in a quiet, weedy area, one or the other

A school of hungry piranhas feasts on the flesh of a capybara, a large rodent (inset) that dwells in the Amazon.

of the parents will guard the nest. Anyone who accidentally wades near one of these nests stands a strong chance of being bitten. Protective piranhas do not attack in groups, only individually. The result is often a single, circular, slow-healing bite.

A lone piranha guards its nest, ready to attack anything that comes too close to it.

Piranhas may not be the human-devouring monsters of legend. But they are capable of inflicting tremendous damage. People have suffered painful wounds from encounters with the fish. Given these facts and the many mysteries that remain about piranhas, people have little choice but to be wary of these razor-toothed fish.

Chapter 1

Piranha Attacks in the Wild

The first Europeans to enter the Amazon rain forests were Spanish explorers and soldiers in the sixteenth century. Some of the most gruesome stories of piranha attacks came from these startled visitors.

These included reports of a member of their own exploring party being eaten alive while wading in the river. One monk traveling with the group also told of a hostile encounter with native people who lived in the rain forest. The Spanish shot some of the natives, who fell out of their canoes into the river and turned up shortly after as skeletons.

There is no way of knowing if these accounts were exaggerated to make the adventure sound

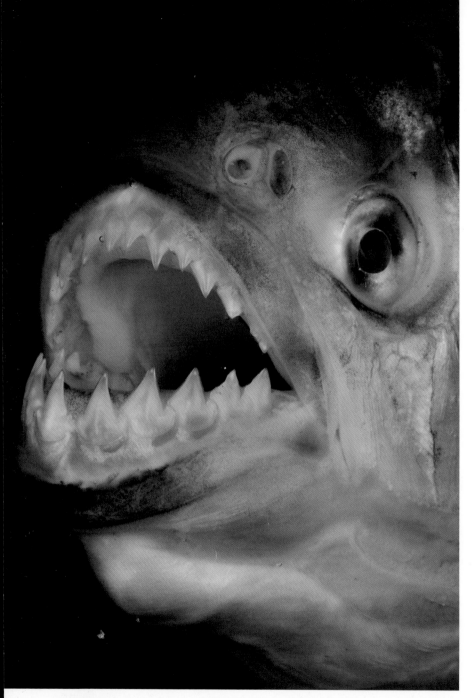

Sixteenth-century Spanish explorers in the Amazon were terrified of the ferocious piranha, shown here close-up.

more interesting to the folks back home. Experience with piranhas in modern times shows that such attacks are not typical.

Nonetheless, piranhas are capable of doing such damage, and experts give two possible explanations for these unusually violent incidents. First, battle injuries among both the Spanish and their foes would have put an unusual amount of blood in the water. Such an excess of blood could easily provoke feeding frenzies among piranhas. Second, many of the Spaniard soldiers wore red pants as part of their uniform. Piranhas are known to become aggressive around that color. In fact, fishers in some areas use bits of red cloth as well as red meat as bait when fishing for piranhas.

Deep Scars

In the early 1800s a more highly trained observer arrived on the scene. Alexander von Humboldt, one of the greatest scientific explorers of his time, spent some years in the Amazon rain forest. He reported that piranhas were dangerous, but not deadly.

The piranha "attacks bathers and swimmers from whom it carries away considerable portions of flesh,"[3] he wrote. "When a person is only slightly wounded, it is difficult for him to get out of the water without a severe wound. . . . Several of [the Indians] showed us the scars of deep wounds in the calf or leg or on the thighs, made by these little animals."[4]

Attacks in the River

Theodore Roosevelt wrote that piranhas "will snap a finger off a hand incautiously trailed in the water."[5] Most of the stories of piranha attacks that he gathered while on his Amazon trip came from the Brazilian explorer Candido Rondon. On one occasion, Rondon went to the river's edge to bathe. He carefully inspected a clear, shallow pool near the bank to make sure no piranhas were there. But no sooner did he step into the water than a piranha attacked and bit off his toe.

On another occasion, one of Rondon's men was wading in the river when a piranha bit him on the upper leg. When the man put his hands in the water to protect the wound, a mass of fish attacked. The man escaped further injury by jumping up onto an overhanging branch, but the painful wounds took six months to heal.

The most frightening of Rondon's stories was the case of a member of his group who went off by himself for a while on a mule. The mule returned; the man did not. The rest of the party followed the mule's trail until they came to a skeleton near the shore of the river. They could find no logical explanation other than that he had encountered piranhas.

Piranha Attack or Not?

Such gruesome reports are not unknown in modern times. Harald Schultz, who spent twenty years

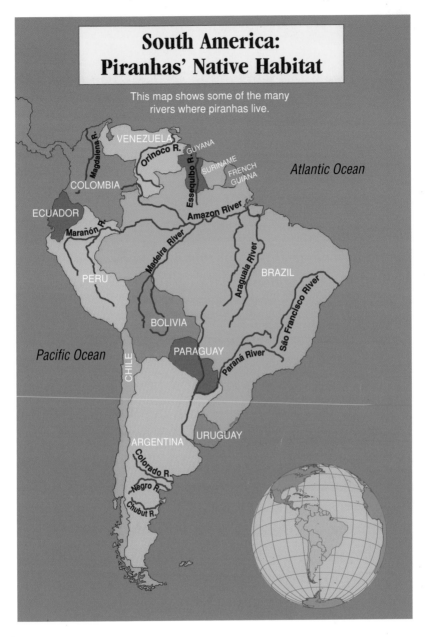

South America: Piranhas' Native Habitat

This map shows some of the many rivers where piranhas live.

VENEZUELA
GUYANA
Orinoco R.
SURINAME
Essequibo R.
FRENCH GUIANA
Magdalena R.
COLOMBIA
Atlantic Ocean
ECUADOR
Amazon River
Marañón R.
Madeira River
PERU
Araguaia River
BRAZIL
São Francisco River
BOLIVIA
Pacific Ocean
PARAGUAY
CHILE
Paraná River
ARGENTINA
URUGUAY
Colorado R.
Negro R.
Chubut R.

studying in the Amazon rain forest, knows of a similar case. "I did hear of one boy whose boat capsized in the middle of a river and who became the victim of piranhas,"[6] reported Schultz.

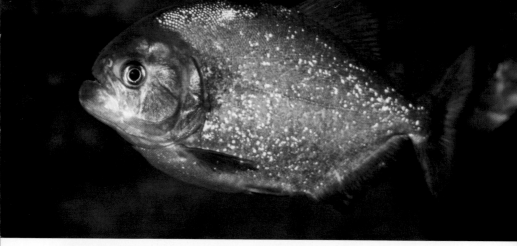

Piranhas play an important role in the environment by devouring dead animals that might otherwise spread disease.

The question that remains unanswered in both this case and the one Roosevelt reported was, did piranhas attack the victim? Or had the boy suffered a heart attack, or fallen and drowned? Piranhas are known for devouring dead bodies in the river. In fact, they perform an important service by disposing of rotting flesh in a hot, wet climate that would otherwise promote the spread of disease. Piranha experts suspect that in the few cases where **skeletonized** bodies have been found in rivers, the persons were dead before the piranhas attacked. Such a claim, however, is impossible to prove either way.

Unpredictable

Many South Americans who have lived around piranhas all their lives have no particular fear of them. In most rivers where piranhas live, attacks are so rare that people routinely swim, wade, and bathe among the fish without a second thought. But just because attacks are rare does not mean that the fish can be taken for granted. In twenty years of exploration, Harald Schultz met seven people who had been attacked by piranhas, one of them seriously. According to one experienced guide, people who swim in piranha-infested waters run a good risk of getting bitten at some time or other.

Looking for Trouble

Nonetheless, by far the majority of piranha attacks are **provoked** by people who go out of their way to encounter the fish. Most of these people are fishing guides and their customers. Piranhas are tasty,

A Yawalapiti boy swims in an Amazonian river without fear of being bitten by piranhas.

and they make up an important part of people's diet in parts of the Amazon rain forest. Also, their fierce reputation makes them a tempting target for tourists looking for a touch of adventure.

A piranha, which might pose no threat to someone swimming nearby in a river, suddenly becomes dangerous when it feels threatened. As piranha expert Barry Chernoff notes, "When you catch them in nets or on a hook and line, they're not happy to see you."[7]

Avoiding Piranha Attacks in the Wild

Despite the unpredictable nature of piranhas, people can reduce the chances of being attacked. The most obvious way is to avoid going in the water with a fresh wound or open sore. Blood can attract and excite piranhas from a great distance. When

Fishers in the Amazon basin risk having their catch eaten by hungry piranhas.

piranhas smell blood, if just one decides to attack, it could set off a feeding frenzy among the others. The effect that blood has on piranhas is also a good reason for staying away from areas of the river routinely used for cleaning fish or disposing of fish guts. Piranhas may become conditioned to feeding in such an area and be more likely to attack.

Anyone swimming in waters known to have piranhas should avoid wild splashing or thrashing. That type of movement appears to attract and excite piranhas. Fishers in piranha-infested waters often find their catch attacked and devoured before they can land the fish. This is because the hooked fish **instinctively** thrash and so attract piranhas.

Swimmers and waders also have a better chance of avoiding piranhas if they stay in clear water. Most piranha attacks occur in shallow, muddy areas where the fish do not have a clear picture of what they might be attacking.

Piranhas should be avoided during dry seasons, especially when stranded in evaporating pools of water. Piranhas in such a situation are probably starving. A piranha is strong enough to leap well out of the water if it senses food nearby. The fish are also best avoided during their spawning season.

Finally, any piranha caught by hook or by net should be treated with extreme caution. Trapped piranhas are likely to snap at anything that moves.

Chapter 3

Piranha Attacks in Captivity

Piranhas are celebrities of the animal world. Almost everyone has heard of them and their ferocious reputation. People are as curious about these famous fish as they are afraid of them. Something about seeing such a dreaded creature up close fascinates both young and old. As a result, piranhas are popular attractions at aquariums. Exotic fish dealers do a brisk business selling them as pets.

Piranhas, however, cannot be tamed. They must be treated with great care at all times. Piranha pet owners, aquarium visitors, and even expert fish handlers who forget this rule risk losing a piece of their finger. Piranhas are such powerful swimmers that they can strike and be gone before the victim can react to them. They can leap out of water. Their jaws snap shut faster than the blinking of an eye. Their teeth are so sharp that victims often lose chunks of flesh before they feel the bite. The bites are relatively small, because piranhas are small. But they can inflict permanent damage and even require **amputation** of a finger.

Toddler's Surprise

Injuries from piranhas in captivity are usually the result of ignorance or carelessness. Small children and captured piranhas can be a dangerous mix. In June 2004, an eighteen-month-old girl was visiting the Butterfly and Insect World in Edinburgh, Scotland. Among the attractions that drew 13,000 children a year to visit the place was a tank filled with

Yawalapiti Indian boys show off the large, jagged teeth of a piranha they caught in a river in Brazil.

a close cousin of the piranha called the pacu. These fish do not normally eat meat and are considered far safer than piranhas.

As a safety feature, the fish were kept in a large tank with sides that rose 3.5 feet (1.1m) off the ground. Yet the child was lifted up to get a look. No one noticed the girl dangling her arm over the water. Suddenly, the girl shrieked and pulled her hand away. Attached to it was a small fish. Drops of her blood falling into the water sent other fish into such a frenzy that some of them leaped clear out of the tank.

Staff members raced to the girl's aid and removed the fish. She was rushed to a hospital, where emergency **plastic surgery** was performed to save her finger.

Carelessness

The little girl obviously did not know better than to put her hand there. But there are many cases where people who know what piranhas can do forget to treat the fish with respect.

A reporter described a case near the Rio Paraua in Venezuela of an experienced fishing guide who let his guard down. The guide had a vat filled with small piranhas that he used to bait hooks to catch a larger fish called the vampire fish. He enjoyed scaring his guests with his fearless behavior. Every once in a while, he would put his hand in the water and then shriek as if he had been attacked. As a joke, he once attached a dead piranha to his finger as he

A biologist at the Manila airport in the Philippines confiscates baby piranhas from a passenger's luggage.

howled in mock pain, and then laughed at his audience's horror.

But he quickly found that piranhas are not to be treated lightly. In the reporter's words, "I watched as he chased an **elusive** fish round and round the bait tank. Then he yanked his hand away and winced." The reporter never saw the fish or the lightning-fast attack. "Then I noticed the blood on the index finger of his right hand."[8] The guide was missing a fingertip, including part of the fingernail.

Biting the Hand That Feeds

Even expert fish handlers who take precautions when dealing with piranhas find that they are not always safe from an attack. Dr. Frederick Aldrich, a biology researcher, came back from an expedition to the Amazon with some red-bellied piranhas, one

The red-bellied piranha is especially dangerous and aggressive, attacking its prey with lightning speed.

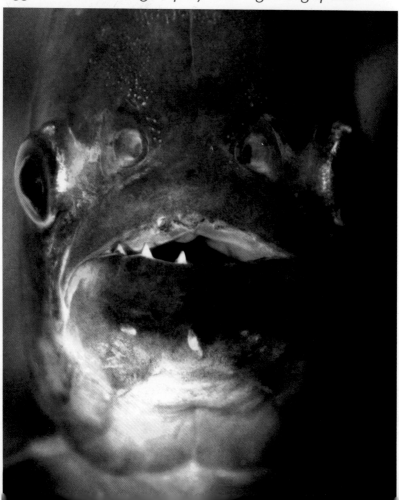

of the fiercest varieties. One of his assistants, Matt, carefully used a dip net to fish out a couple of the piranhas. As Aldrich describes it, "One of the little red-bellied beauties flipped and seemed to bounce off Matt's hand as he held the handle of the net and fell back into the water, now turned red."[9] Again, the attack was so swift that no one actually saw the bite. But when Matt held up his finger, there was a bleeding, circular, 1-inch (2.5cm) hole in it.

Helle Hogner was doing nothing dangerous as she performed her duties at Reptile Park in Oslo, Norway, in December 2004. Well-trained in the ways of the piranha, she opened the hatch on the piranha tank to show some visitors how they fed the fish. Her hand was nowhere near the water when one of the fish leaped high in the air and snapped at her hand. The bite was so quick and clean that Hogner never felt a thing. But blood be-gan spurting from the trademark circular bite, and she had to go the emergency room for treatment.

Problems with Pet Owners

It is impossible to say how many pet owners suffer a similar fate. Piranhas are illegal in many parts of the world and more than half of the United States. Those illegally keeping the fish are likely to avoid treatment for a bite rather than admit their crime.

But pet fish are believed to be responsible for some public attacks on unsuspecting people. In August 2004, a fourteen-year-old boy was playing

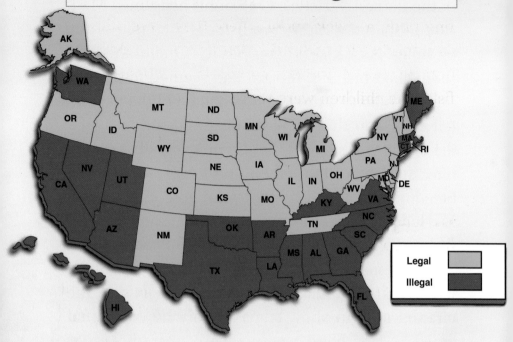

Where Piranhas Are Legal as Pets

Legal
Illegal

in a public fountain near a housing complex in Hong Kong, China. Along with three of his friends, he spotted some fish swimming about and tried to catch one. Before he realized what happened, he found himself staring at a hole in one of his fingers that oozed blood into the pool.

The boy was taken to a hospital, where he needed three stitches to close the wound. Authorities, meanwhile, could not catch the quick-swimming fish. In the morning, they drained the fountain completely and found three fish, two of which were piranhas. Experts were certain that the fish were once pets that had been abandoned by their owners.

Children in Berlin, Germany, narrowly avoided what could have been an even worse situation a few years ago. A group of kids was playing in a petting pool, a special pool where they were allowed to wade in and touch the fish. Suddenly someone noticed one of the fish starting to attack the other fish. The children were removed, and the pool was drained. Sure enough, the attacking fish was a piranha, most likely another abandoned pet.

Avoiding Piranha Attacks in Captivity

Most problems with piranhas in captivity can be avoided by observing strict safety rules. The most important of these is that small children should never be allowed near the fish. Hands should be kept as far

Captive piranhas kept in aquariums will often eat any other fish that share their tank.

away from the aquarium as possible at all times. Like trainers of poisonous snakes and other dangerous animals, piranha handlers run a risk simply by the nature of their job. The occasional attack is probably unavoidable, but the risk can be lessened by always respecting the damage that these fish can do.

The dangers of piranhas showing up where they are not expected are the responsibility of pet owners. Experts say that too many people buy piranhas as a novelty. Before long, they tire of the trouble of feeding them, of seeing piranhas destroy other valuable fish in the tank, or of the precautions they need to take around them. Thinking that it would be cruel to kill the piranhas, they drop them in a river, lake, pond, or fountain. In solving their personal problem, they create a danger for others. No piranha should ever be released outside its native environment.

Chapter 4

New Dangers

Over the past century, piranha attacks have been a minor nuisance, not a serious problem. In their natural environment, these fish have largely avoided people. Seldom, if ever, have they unleashed the lethal attacks on humans of which they are capable. If left undisturbed, there is reason to respect piranhas but not fear them.

Unfortunately, piranhas are not being left alone in their natural environment. Human tinkering has already created situations that have greatly increased piranha attacks. This interference has the potential of creating even greater problems in the future.

Human encounters with piranhas typically occur in shallow, muddy water where the fish cannot see what they are attacking.

Outbreak of Piranha Attacks

A small population of speckled and dark-brown piranhas has lived in the Rio Mogi Guacci in southeastern Brazil for many years. Until recently, reports of piranha attacks on humans were rare.

That changed drastically in 1999. Suddenly, dozens of people were jumping out of the water with blood streaming from small wounds. The injuries were almost always the same—a single, round, crater-shaped wound about 1 inch (2.5cm) in diameter, usually on the legs or feet. The attacks almost always struck people wading near the shore, in shallow, muddy water.

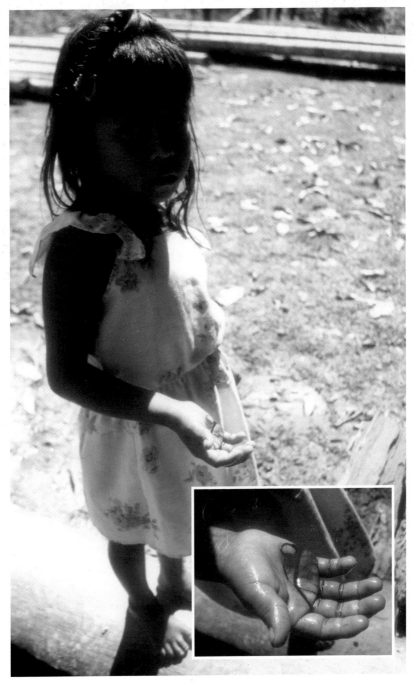

This Brazilian girl was bitten by a piranha while taking fish out of a net.

In late 2002, 38 such attacks were recorded over a period of five weekends near Santa Cruz of Conceiçao, a town with a population of 3,500. A similar rash of attacks hit two other nearby towns, neither of which had experienced piranha problems before. At the peak of the outbreak, more than 50 piranha attacks took place in the area during a two-week period. One of the injuries was so severe that the toe had to be amputated.

A Human-Made Problem

The rash of piranha attacks in the area had nothing to do with a change in the piranhas' behavior. Rather, it was human behavior that created the problem. The most important of these changes was the introduction of dams in the rivers. The three areas with the greatest increase in piranha attacks all happened to be near new dams. The dams were put in place to control the flow of the rivers. By controlling the river flow, the authorities would be able to prevent flooding that was causing hardship for the growing population.

As Brazilian zoologist Ivan Sazima noted, "When you dam a river, you create ideal conditions for the piranha population to rise."[10] Piranhas prefer slow-moving waters for their spawning grounds. They particularly like to lay their eggs in submerged or floating water weeds, such as the water hyacinth. In a swift-flowing river, such weeds are unable to grow. Even in stretches where they do grow, they

Tourists like these on a rafting trip along a river in Brazil are at risk for a potentially harmful encounter with a piranha.

are often swept away by the high, fast waters when the river floods. The dams, however, stopped the flooding, which allowed the piranhas' favorite weeds to stay in place and thrive. Experts believe the new conditions increased the piranha population to more than ten times its former level.

At the same time, the dams created quiet stretches of river ideal for recreation. The growing human population of the area flocked to these areas to swim and wade during the hot summer months. The swimming was so good that the area soon attracted large numbers of tourists.

A Dangerous Mix

The exploding population of piranhas in contact with the growing number of humans using the rivers created a dangerous situation. The situation grew even worse because of the timing. Late summer is an especially popular time for water recreation. That is exactly the time when piranhas tend to breed. During this time, piranhas are particularly aggressive. Either one of the parents may stand guard, protecting the spawning site. They are likely to attack anything that approaches the nest.

With the greatest number of people entering the river at exactly the time when dense populations of

A fisherman poses with the piranha he caught in the Cuyahoga River in Ohio. The fish was probably an abandoned pet.

piranhas were at their most aggressive stage, trouble was inevitable. The vast majority of the attacks targeted people wading in the river near a piranha nest.

The lesson of the Rio Mogi Guacci outbreak is that human behavior can create dangers where none existed. Continued damming of rivers and increased use of piranha-infested waters for recreation create an environment ripe for piranha attacks.

Being Alert

People can reduce the chances of attacks by being alert to the situation. Most of the piranha attacks in southeastern Brazil occurred where signs were posted warning of the danger of piranhas.

On a larger scale, people can study the effects of dams and try to reduce the impact they have on piranha habitat. Where dams are necessary, some precautions can be taken to protect people from unfortunate encounters with piranhas. On quiet rivers, water weeds could be cleaned out every so often to reduce spawning habitat of the fish. Nets could be set up to separate swimming areas from aggressive spawning piranhas.

Spread of Piranhas

Piranhas are warm-water fish that thrive only in the remote rain forests of South America. In this restricted habitat, among people who are familiar with them, the fish pose only a limited danger.

Since at least the 1990s, however, piranhas have been turning up all over the globe. Fishers in the United States have caught piranhas in many states, including Nebraska, Iowa, Connecticut, Pennsylvania, Florida, and Utah. In 2003, two piranhas were captured in the same week, just a few miles from each other near Warren, Ohio. These are just the confirmed cases; many other fishers tell stories of catching these razor-toothed fish.

Nor is the spread of piranhas restricted to the United States. This tropical fish has been captured as far north as a Canadian lake. In 2003, piranhas were caught in the Czech Republic and Vietnam. In August 2004, piranhas were found in both the Netherlands and Spain.

The Unexpected

There is no doubt that the spread of piranhas is due to the brisk trade in the fish among pet dealers and owners. The fish are then abandoned by owners who tire of caring for them.

The spread of piranhas in this way poses a number of concerns. First, the appearance of a razor-toothed fish that is not supposed to be in an area can pose a danger. Unsuspecting fishers from Johnson Creek, Oregon, to the Volga region of Russia have been bitten by piranhas they hooked. A wound from a single piranha, however, is only a minor danger. Since piranhas are not believed to be able to survive the winters of most climates, the

A Chinese official holds a piranha he seized from a pet market. The fish will be destroyed to keep it from entering the local ecosystem.

problem of abandoned fish would seem to be short-lived in most places.

What If Piranhas Adapt?

But there is concern about the possibility that piranhas could thrive in new environments. Florida, for example, has a climate that piranhas would thrive in. China has seen evidence that piranhas are living in its Yellow River. Some believe that piranhas could eventually adapt to even colder environments. Noting a series of piranhas caught in western Iowa, some people question whether all of them could have been released pets. For every fish caught, dozens likely remain uncaught. This led one reporter to joke, "If these are released pets, there must be a piranha unloading ramp to accommodate"[11] all that exist in the Missouri River.

Furthermore, a piranha was discovered in the Mississippi River in Minneapolis, Minnesota, near a **warm-water discharge**. Such heated water areas could provide an environment in which piranhas could survive winters.

The danger with spreading piranhas is that no one knows what to expect when a species is introduced to an area where it has no enemies. If piranhas adapt to a new environment, their population numbers could explode. Given the problems this meat-eating fish could cause, many countries, and many states in the United States, ban piranhas within their borders. Whether they can enforce the ban is an open question. But all agree that caution is the best strategy to prevent piranhas from being a greater problem in the future.

Notes

Chapter 1: Deadliest Fish or Fake Monster?

1. Roger Caras, *Dangerous to Man*. New York: Holt, Rinehart and Winston, 1975, p. 259.

2. Quoted in Per Olda and Emily d'Aulaire, "Piranha!" *International Wildlife*, May 1986, p. 31.

Chapter 2: Piranha Attacks in the Wild

3. Quoted in Wolfgang Schulte, *Piranhas in the Aquarium*. Neptune City, NJ: THF Publications, 1988, p. 9.

4. Quoted in Christine Chrzanowski, "Alexander von Humboldt and the Casiquiara River," December 7, 2000. www.members.aol.com/Chris Chrz/humboldt.html.

5. Quoted in Caras, *Dangerous to Man*, p. 257.

6. Quoted in Bernard Grzimek, ed., *Fishes: Grzimek's Animal Life Encyclopedia,* vol. 4. New York: Von Nostrand Reinhold, 1973, p. 2,834.

7. Barry Chernoff, "In His Own Words," *Discovery,* July 4, 2004, p. 62.

Chapter 3: Piranha Attacks in Captivity

8. Keith Sutton, "Out There: Piranha!" ESPN Outdoors.com, 2005. www.espn.go.com/out doors/general/columns/sutton_keith/1411436. html.

9. Frederick Aldrich, "Sciencefare: April 15, 1982." www.mun.ca/sgs/science/april1582.html.

Chapter 4: New Dangers

10. Quoted in Paul Rincon, "Piranha Increase 'Due to Dams,'" BBC News, December 28, 2003. www.news.bbc.co.uk/2/hi/science/nature/ 3346301.stm.

11. Roger Welsh, "Jaws," *Natural History*, August 1996, p. 67.

Glossary

aggressive: A trait of attacking rather than ignoring or running away.

amputation: Removal of a body part when it cannot be saved or repaired.

elusive: Difficult to catch.

feeding frenzy: Wild, uncontrolled eating.

instinctively: Taking an action without having to think about it because of a built-in sense of what should be done.

plastic surgery: An operation to make an injured or abnormal part of the body look as normal as possible.

provoked: Taking some sort of action that causes a reaction in turn.

rain forests: Areas of wet, hot climate that produce tremendous growth of plant life.

skeletonized: Having all tissue removed so that only bone remains.

species: Groups of individual animals or plants that are so much alike that they can be defined as being separate from all other groups.

warm-water discharge: Waste water, often from a factory or electrical plant, that is released into the environment.

For Further Exploration

Book

Wolfgang Schulte, *Piranhas in the Aquarium*. Neptune City, NJ: THF Publications, 1988. A slightly dated but well-written and complete study of piranhas, including their history, anatomy, and behavior, as well as information on raising piranhas (where it is legal to do so).

Periodical

Paul A. Zabel, "Seeking the Truth About the Feared Piranha," *National Geographic,* November 1975. A balanced look at how the piranha got its reputation and whether that reputation is deserved.

Internet Sources

Frank Magallamus, "Legendary Myth of Piranha Revealed." www.angelfire.com/biz/piranha038/mythpira.html. A fascinating account of how Theodore Roosevelt's hosts on his Amazon expedition staged the feeding frenzy most responsible for spreading the piranhas' fierce reputation.

———, "The Piranha in Truth." http://home.nyc.rr com/pita/truth.htm. A leading expert on piranhas offers information on piranhas in the wild and then explores some of the advantages, disadvantages, and legal aspects of owning the fish as a pet.

Popular Mechanics, "Worst-Case Scenarios: How to Cross a Piranha-Infested River." www.popularme chanics.com/science/worst_case_scenario/ 1289301.html. A brief primer on the best way to protect against a piranha attack in the wild.

Web Sites

Aquaria Central (www.aquariacentral.com/arti cles/bpiranha.shtml). In this site a piranha owner talks about his first-hand experiences through the years as an owner of pet piranhas.

Jungle Photos (www.junglephotos.com). A fun Web site filled with photographs of the different piranha species, piranha skulls, teeth, and other features. It also has some historical information.

The Red-Bellied Piranha (http://pubpages. unh.edu/~sahutz). A useful site that focuses on the red-bellied piranha. It includes photos that show the growth of a pet piranha, instructions for setting up an aquarium for piranhas, and answers to frequently asked questions about the fish.

Index

Picture Credits

About the Author

Nathan Aaseng has written more than 170 books, many of them for young readers. He holds a degree in biology and English from Luther College and was honored as Wisconsin Notable Author in 1999.